STEPPING INTO SCIENCE

HOW BIG IS A STICK?

By Illa Podendorf

Illustrations by Richard Mlodock

CHILDRENS PRESS, CHICAGO

Illa Podendorf, former Chairman of the Science Department of the Laboratory Schools, University of Chicago, has prepared this series of books with emphasis on the processes of science. The content is selected from the main branches of science—biology, physics, and chemistry—but the thrust is on the process skills which are essential in scientific work. Some of the processes emphasized are observing, classifying, communicating, measuring, inferring, and predicting. The treatment is intellectually stimulating which makes it occupy an active part in a child's thinking. This is important in all general education of children.

This book stresses the process of measuring. It offers opportunities for experience with arbitrary units of measure and points up the necessity for standard units.

Copyright © 1971 by Regensteiner Publishing Enterprises, Inc.
All rights reserved. Published simultaneously in Canada.
Printed in the United States of America

Library of Congress Catalog Card Number: 75-148585

5 6 7 8 9 10 11 12 13 14 15 16 17 18 19 20 21 22 23 24 25 R 75 74

CONTENTS

How Long Are Sticks? 4

How Big Around Are
   Sticks? 16

How Long Is a
   Crooked Stick? 30

How Long Is a Tall Stick? 32

How Are Sticks The Same? 40

How Are Sticks
   Different? 43

Things To Do 48

HOW LONG ARE STICKS?

Andy and Jerry found a stick.
They thought it was a long stick.

It was longer than their dog, Duff.

It was longer than Andy.

They gave it a name.
They called it *Jerry Stick*.

Jerry and Andy hunted more sticks. None of them were as long as the one they called *Jerry Stick*.

They put their sticks in a row,
in an order.
Can you find the *Jerry Stick?*
Can you see what the order is?

One stick was as long as Andy's arm.

It was shorter than Jerry's arm.

They called it the *Andy Arm Stick.*

One stick was about as long as Andy's leg.

It was shorter than Jerry's leg.

They called it the *Andy Leg Stick*.

11

One of the sticks was only as long as Jerry's hand.
   They called it the *Jerry Hand Stick*.

One of the sticks was about as long as their dog, Duff.
They called it the *Duff Dog Stick*.

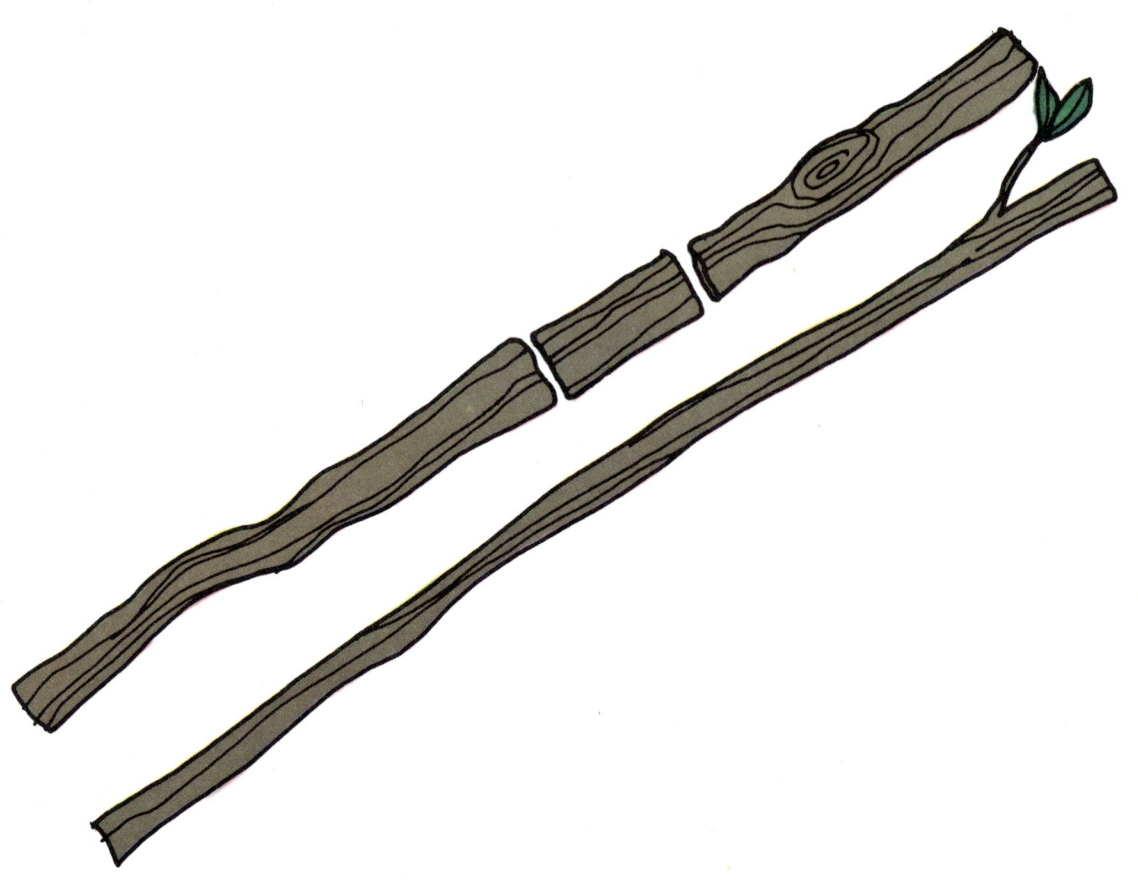

It took three of the sticks to be as long as the *Jerry Stick*.

They were the *Duff Dog Stick*, the *Jerry Hand Stick*, and the *Andy Arm Stick*.

Jerry and Andy found that it took almost two of the *Andy Leg Sticks* to be as long as the *Jerry Stick.*

HOW BIG AROUND ARE STICKS?

The boys noticed something more.

They noticed that some sticks were bigger around than others.

The *Andy Leg Stick* was about as big around as Andy's wrist.

They thought of giving it another name. They might call it the *Andy Wrist Stick*.

They decided that two names for the same stick was not such a good idea.

The *Andy Arm Stick* was about as big around as Duff's tail.

One of the sticks was not a long one, but
it was about as big around as Andy's fist.

They put their sticks in a row in an order. Can you see what the order is, this time?

The boys made another discovery.

They could not use the *Jerry Stick,* the *Andy Arm Stick,* or the *Duff Dog Stick* to measure around the sticks.

Jerry had an idea.

He would hold string around the sticks, and then find out how long the string was.

He got a piece of string and put it around the *Andy Leg Stick*.
It worked fine. The string was as long as the *Jerry Hand Stick*.

The boys found a big, thick stick.

The string was too short to go around it.

Andy used his shoelace to measure around the big, thick stick.

The part of the shoelace that went around the stick was longer than the *Jerry Hand Stick,* and shorter than the *Andy Arm Stick.*

The boys' father came along.

"I can help you," he said. "I can get you some rulers. Rulers are useful when you want to find the size of things. Many people in the United States use rulers with inches on them. But people in most countries, and all scientists, use rulers with centimeters on them. Centimeters are used in the metric system of measuring."

Jerry said, "Then we would like rulers with centimeters on them."

The boys' father gave them two rulers. One was short, and one was longer.

The short ruler was about as long as Andy's hand. It is called a *decimeter* ruler. A decimeter ruler has ten centimeters on it.

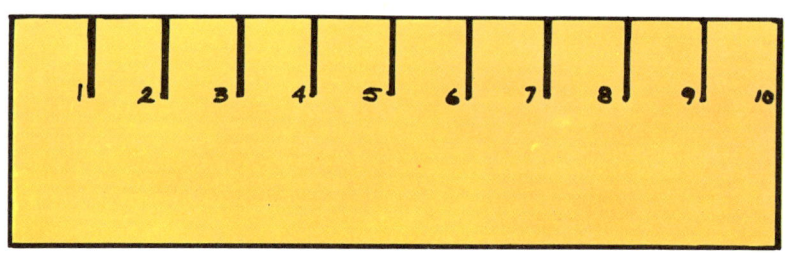

The longer ruler was one meter long.
A meter is made of 10 decimeters, or 100 centimeters.
The meter ruler was about as long as Andy from his toes to his chin.

Now the boys could use a ruler to find how long their sticks were.

They could find how big around they were by measuring the string with a ruler.

HOW LONG IS A CROOKED STICK?

Andy had a straight stick. He stood it up. Jerry had a crooked stick. He stood it up. "My stick is longer than your stick," said Andy.

"Let's see if it is," said Jerry.

He laid a piece of string along the curves of the crooked stick.

Then he measured the string. He could see that his crooked stick would be longer than Andy's straight one, if it were straight, too.

HOW LONG IS A TALL STICK?

Andy found a stick that was about as long as he was tall.

Now both Jerry and Andy had sticks that were about as long as they were tall.

"If we hold them up tall, they are as tall as we are," said Jerry.

"Then the sticks will be the same as each other," said Andy.

But were they?

Andy found another stick that was as long as he was tall.

Now will his two sticks be the same length?

Look at the picture.

35

Andy saw a shadow on the ground.
He found a stick that was as long
as the shadow.

He measured the shadow. It was one meter long.
How long was the stick?

Andy measured two sticks.

One was standing up, and one was flat on the ground.

Each of them was two decimeters long.

Jerry found a third stick.
It was just as long
as one of the two
Andy had measured.
Is the third stick two
decimeters long, too?
Are all three sticks
the same length?

HOW ARE STICKS THE SAME?

Andy took a careful look at all the sticks. He noticed some things about them.

He said, "It's easy to see that they all have length. And if they are straight sticks, they stand as tall as they are long."

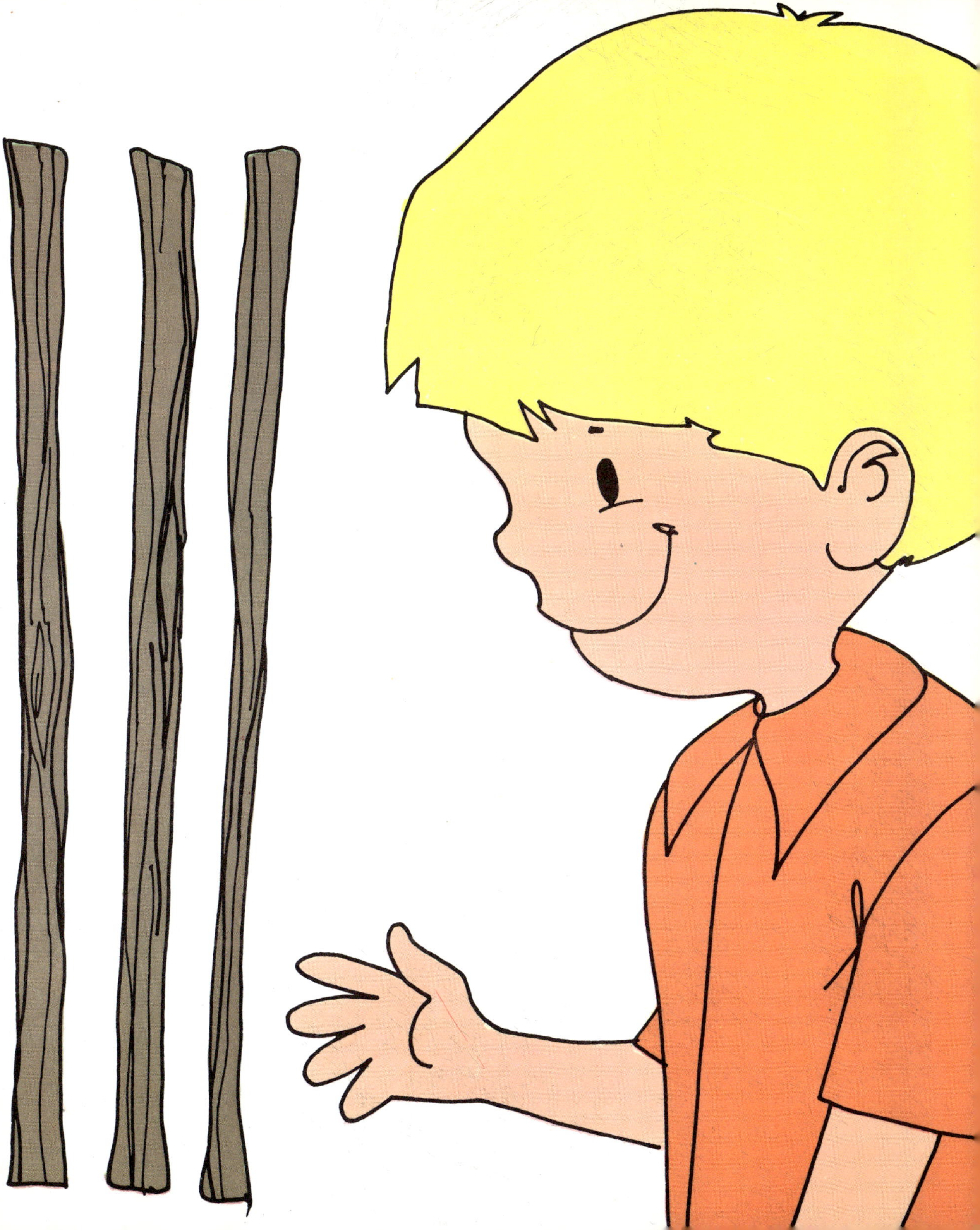

Then Andy said, "All sticks have a distance around them that we can measure."

HOW ARE STICKS DIFFERENT?

Both boys knew that sticks have differences.

Sticks have different lengths.

43

Longer sticks stand taller than shorter sticks.

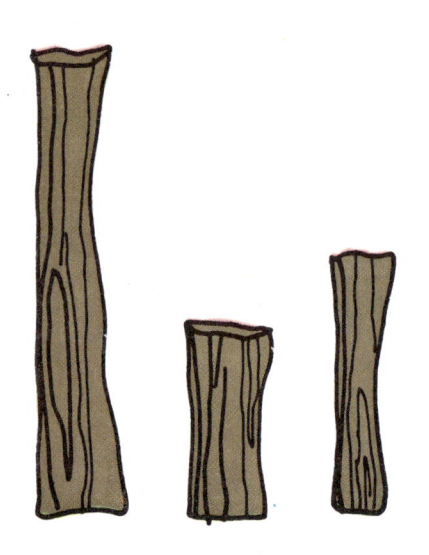

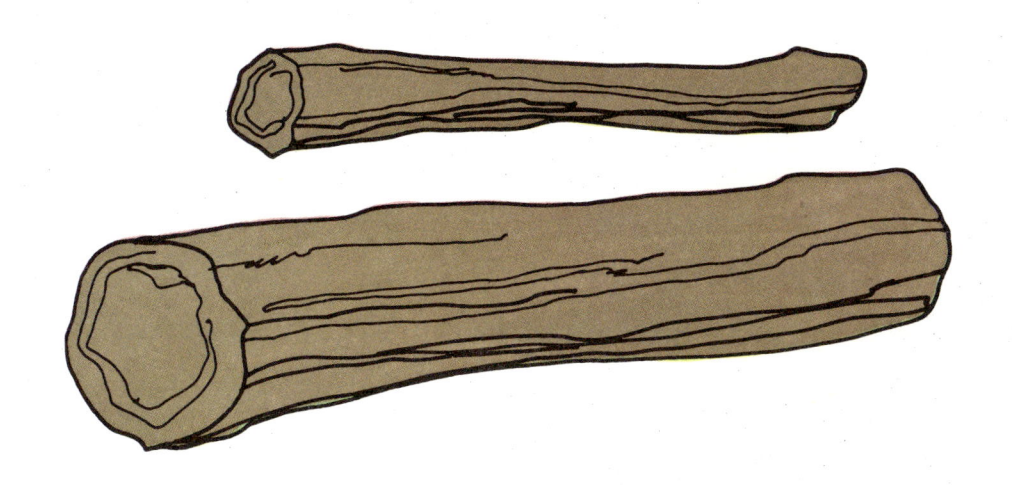

Some sticks are bigger around than others.

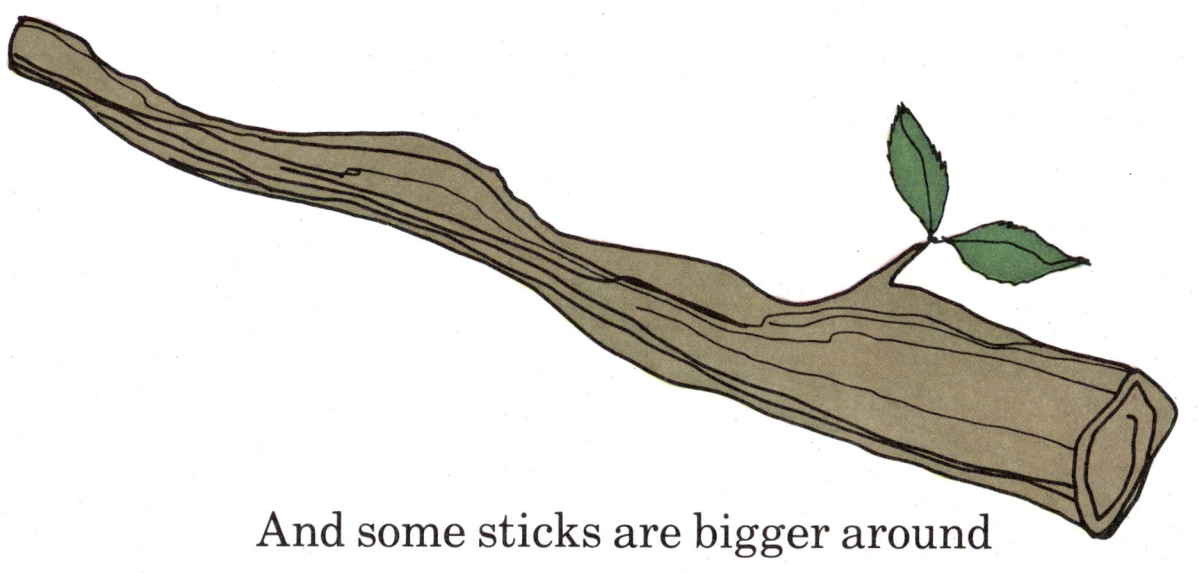

And some sticks are bigger around at some places than at others.

Some sticks are crooked. Crooked sticks do not stand up as tall as they would if they were straight.

One of these sticks is more crooked than the other.

It looks shorter because it is more crooked.

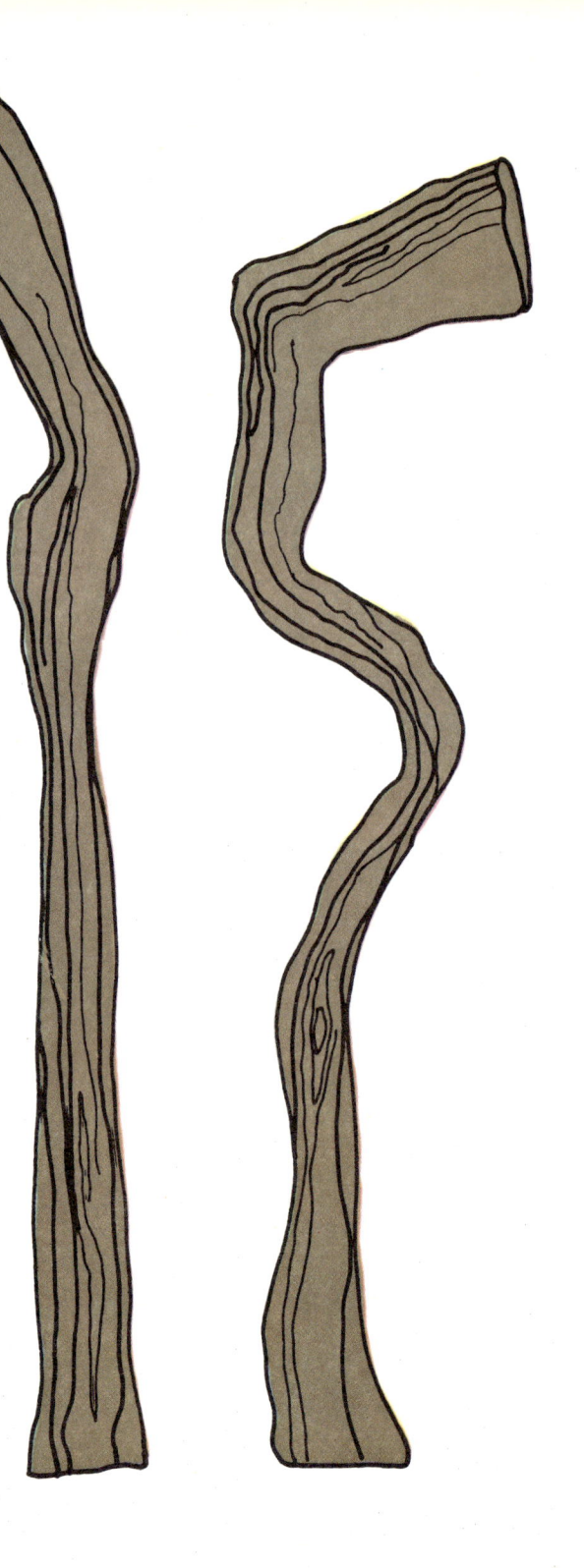

Jerry and Andy had so many sticks that they built a cabin with them.

THINGS TO DO

Go on a stick hunt and find as many as you can.

How many of them were the same length?

Did you have one as long as you are tall?

Use a ruler to find how long each of the sticks really is.

Did you find a crooked stick that was about as long as a straight stick?

Try to find a stick that is as long as your favorite toy.

Are any of the sticks as big around as your wrist?

Did you find a stick that was so long and big around that you could not lift it?

See what you can build with your sticks.

HENRY H. HOUSTON PUBLIC SCHOOL

ALLEN AND RURAL LANES

PHILADELPHIA, PA. 19119

LIBRARY

11,266

389
POD   Podendorf, Illa

How big is a stick?

DATE DUE